31 Affirmations for the Proverbs 31 Women

Dr. Latina C. Campbell

ISBN: 978-1-955312-54-7

Printed in the United States of America
Story Corner Publishing & Consulting, Inc.
3810 Indian River Rd. Suite 13031
Chesapeake, VA 23325

Storycornerpublishing@yahoo.com

www.StoryCornerPublishing.com

DEDICATION

I dedicate this book to every woman trying to find her way through life. You can make it if you faint not!

TABLE OF CONTENTS

INTRODUCTION

King Solomon was the wisest man of his time, and he gave us the outline of the ideal woman in Proverbs chapter 31. He makes it clear that she pursues the wisdom of God instead of the corrupt wisdom of the world. The Proverbs 31 woman is a virtuous woman who is not concerned with what seems right according to society. Instead, she focuses on God's truth which is His Word. Her biggest desire is to honor God in every way. The Proverbs 31 woman is also a wife, mother, and entrepreneur. She attracts favor from the Lord and is the favor presented to her husband. She is also wise, humble, strong, and gentle. Through her careful business dealings, forward-thinking, competence, tireless work, and strength of character, she enhances the family's dignity, adds esteem to her husband's reputation, and is deeply loved by her entire household. Above all else, this is a woman who loves and fears the Lord. A man who finds a wife of such extraordinary worth most certainly obtains a favor from the Lord because she is the favor.

The attributes of a good wife or an ideal woman according to Proverbs chapter 31:

She is trustworthy and dependable.

She is wise and discerning.

She is a hard worker and strong.

She is a good manager and diligent.

She is a positive influence and kind.

She cares about her health.

She is faithful to God.

She is a loving mother.

She loves and honors her husband.

She is respected.

She is intelligent.

She is generous.

She is an entrepreneur.

This book is intended to equip women with the tools to renew and transform their minds. Daily affirmations help us to remember we are somebody because God created us in His image and likeness. We also possess the power of God, and when we allow Him to work through us, nothing is impossible. God did not create us by accident. Therefore, we all have a purpose in life according to His Will. We must believe we are unique to God, and He only wants the best for us. Our perspective about ourselves would change once we elevate our faith in God by His Word or biblical scriptures. According to Romans 10:17 KJV, "Consequently, faith comes by hearing, and hearing the Word of God" should be our focus point.

Affirmation:

The action or process of affirming something or being affirmed. Emotional support or encouragement.

Self-care is nice to think about, but let's face it, we are nothing without God (Yahweh). Therefore, we need Him for all things, even to care for ourselves. When we focus on getting our soul and spirit aligned with God's Word, then everything else will fall into alignment. We would be able to love ourselves the way God intended us to, and loving others would be easy. Soul care is the best care, not self-care.

When we pray, fast, and study God's Word, we strengthen our spirits and lock our souls into God's hands. Some people think, "Once saved, always saved," but that is not true. Salvation is a practice of repentance and obedience to God that we should live every day. We could accept salvation today and not make it into Heaven tomorrow if we do not follow God's commands. Salvation transitions us into a new creature with new rules of life to follow, which are in God and no longer of "the world." Following God's commands are also our love language toward Him. The Proverbs 31 woman understands this very clearly because her first assignment is to please God in all her ways. Therefore, soul care is the most important thing you can do for yourself. Self-care techniques such as spa visits, hair appointments, shopping sprees, etc., will pass away because they are not rooted in God. Ladies, we must consciously decide to put God first in our lives.

Women are trained to work twice as hard at everything we do, which depletes our strength quickly. Therefore, affirmations are necessary to encourage us to keep going even when we want to give up. Affirmations are one portion of soul care. They are decrees that ignite the power God gave us on the inside to come alive or burn brighter. Walk in the authority God has given you. If no one encourages you, do it yourself, just as David did. Put God's Word into practice, so you can believe what you read and rise above every weapon that tries to assassinate you, your marriage, your family, and your business.

Speak these affirmations over your life daily. The more you say it, the more you will believe! God only needs us to believe or have faith to move on our behalf. Even if you do not see these things happening in your life, speak them until they happen. With God, all things are possible.

"For as he thinketh in his heart, so is he: Eat and drink, saith he to thee; but his heart is not with thee."
Proverbs 23:7 KJV

"Death and life are in the power of the tongue: and they that love it shall eat the fruit thereof."
Proverbs 18:21 KJV

"Do not conform to the pattern of this world, but be transformed by the renewing of your mind. Then you will be able to test and approve what God's will is—his good, pleasing, and perfect will."
Romans 12:2 NIV

"Now faith is confidence in what we hope for and assurance about what we do not see."
Hebrews 11:1 NIV

"And without faith it is impossible to please God, because anyone who comes to him must believe that he exists and that he rewards those who earnestly seek him."
Hebrews 11:6 NIV

COMMUNICATION

1. My husband and I have effective communication, and we are united.

"Do not let any unwholesome talk come out of your mouths, but only what is helpful for building others up according to their needs, that it may benefit those who listen."
Ephesians 4:29 NIV

"Jesus knew their thoughts and said to them, "Every kingdom divided against itself will be ruined, and every city or household divided against itself will not stand."
Matthew 12:25 NIV

My Thoughts, Expectations, & Results:

_____

_____

_____

_____

_____

BLESSINGS

2. I am blessed because I obey God's Commands.

"All these blessings will come on you and accompany you if you obey the Lord your God: You will be blessed in the city and blessed in the country. The fruit of your womb will be blessed, and the crops of your land and the young of your livestock—the calves of your herds and the lambs of your flocks. Your basket and your kneading trough will be blessed. You will be blessed when you come in and blessed when you go out. The Lord will grant that the enemies who rise up against you will be defeated before you. They will come at you from one direction but flee from you in seven. The Lord will send a blessing on your barns and on everything you put your hand to. The Lord your God will bless you in the land he is giving you. The Lord will establish you as his holy people, as he promised you on oath, if you keep the commands of the Lord your God and walk in obedience to him. Then all the peoples on earth will see that you are called by the name of the Lord, and they will fear you. The Lord will grant you abundant prosperity—in the fruit of your womb, the young of your livestock and the crops of your ground—in the land he swore to your ancestors to give you. The Lord will open the heavens, the storehouse of his bounty, to send rain on your land in season and to bless all the work of your hands. You will lend to many nations but will borrow from none. The Lord will make you the head, not the tail. If you pay attention to the commands of the Lord your God that I give you this day and carefully follow them, you will always be at

the top, never at the bottom. Do not turn aside from any of the commands I give you today, to the right or to the left, following other gods and serving them."
Deuteronomy 28:2-14 NIV

My Thoughts, Expectations, & Results:

_____

_____

_____

_____

_____

PEACE

3. Peace overtakes me because The Lord has promised me this.

"Though the mountains be shaken and the hills be removed, yet my unfailing love for you will not be shaken nor my covenant of peace be removed," says the Lord, who has compassion on you."
Isaiah 54:10 NIV

My Thoughts, Expectations, & Results:

_____

_____

_____

_____

_____

4. I am the wife worth more than rubies.

"A wife of noble character who can find? She is worth far more than rubies. Her husband has full confidence in her and lacks nothing of value. She brings him good, not harm, all the days of her life."
Proverbs 31:10-12NIV

"An excellent woman [one who is spiritual, capable, intelligent, and virtuous], who is he who can find her? Her value is more precious than jewels and her worth is far above rubies or pearls. The heart of her husband trusts in her [with secure confidence], And he will have no lack of gain. She comforts, encourages, and does him only good and not evil All the days of her life."
Proverbs 31:10-12 AMP

"He who finds a wife finds a good thing and obtains favor from the Lord."
Proverbs 18:22 NIV

My Thoughts, Expectations, & Results:

_____

_____

_____

_____

_____

PREPARED FUTURE

5. Me and my family's future is prosperous and already prepared.

"Strength and dignity are her clothing and her position is strong and secure; And she smiles at the future [knowing that she and her family are prepared]."
Proverbs 31:25 AMP

"When it snows, she has no fear for her household; for all of them are clothed in scarlet. She makes coverings for her bed; she is clothed in fine linen and purple."
Proverbs 31:21-22 NIV

My Thoughts, Expectations, & Results:

_____

_____

_____

_____

_____

GODLY MOTHER

6. I am an excellent, nurturing mother that gives my best to my children.

"Her children rise up and call her blessed (happy, prosperous, to be admired); Her husband also, and he praises her, saying, "Many daughters have done nobly, and well [with the strength of character that is steadfast in goodness], But you excel them all."
Proverbs 31:28-2 AMP

My Thoughts, Expectations, & Results:

_____

_____

_____

_____

_____

GOD-FEARING

7. I am a God-fearing woman who loves the Lord with all my heart.

*"Charm and grace are deceptive, and [superficial]
beauty is vain, But a woman who fears the Lord [reverently
worshiping, obeying, serving, and trusting Him with awe-filled
respect], she shall be praised."*
Proverbs 31:30 AMP

My Thoughts, Expectations, & Results:

_____

_____

_____

_____

_____

SUCCESSFUL ENTREPRENEUR

8. I am a successful entrepreneur and faithful steward of our companies.

> *"She considers a field before she buys or accepts it [expanding her business prudently]; With her profits she plants fruitful vines in her vineyard. She equips herself with strength [spiritual, mental, and physical fitness for her God-given task] And makes her arms strong. She sees that her gain is good; Her lamp does not go out, but it burns continually through the night [she is prepared for whatever lies ahead]."*
> **Proverbs 31:16-18 AMP**

> *"She considers a field and buys it; out of her earnings she plants a vineyard. She sets about her work vigorously; her arms are strong for her tasks. She sees that her trading is profitable, and her lamp does not go out at night."*
> **Proverbs 31:16-18 NIV**

My Thoughts, Expectations, & Results:

_____

_____

_____

_____

_____

A DEEPER RELATIONSHIP WITH GOD

9. My relationship with The Lord runs deeper than the ocean.

"Call to Me and I will answer you, and tell you [and even show you] great and mighty things, [things which have been confined and hidden], which you do not know and understand and cannot distinguish."
Jeremiah 33:3AMP

My Thoughts, Expectations, & Results:

_____

_____

_____

_____

_____

ANSWERED PRAYERS

10. God hears my prayers and answers them according to His will for my life.

"This is the [remarkable degree of] confidence which we [as believers are entitled to] have before Him: if we ask anything according to His will, [that is, consistent with His plan and purpose] He hears us. And if we know [for a fact, as indeed we do] that He hears and listens to us in whatever we ask, we [also] know [with settled and absolute knowledge] that we have [granted to us] the requests which we have asked from Him."
1 John 5:14-15 AMP

My Thoughts, Expectations, & Results:

_____

_____

_____

_____

_____

PROTECTION

11. The Lord protects and fights for my family and me.

"He who dwells in the shelter of the Most High will remain secure and rest in the shadow of the Almighty [whose power no enemy can withstand]. I will say of the Lord, "He is my refuge and my fortress, My God, in whom I trust [with great confidence, and on whom I rely]!"
Psalm 91:1-2 AMP

My Thoughts, Expectations, & Results:

_____

_____

_____

_____

_____

FAVOR

12. I am favored, blessed, and the Lord is with me.

"And coming to her, the angel said, "Greetings, favored one! The Lord is with you."
Luke 1:28 AMP

My Thoughts, Expectations, & Results:

_____

_____

_____

_____

_____

PROSPEROUS HUSBAND

13. My husband is anointed, appointed, victorious, prosperous, and called by God to cover, lead, protect, and be my head.

"The Lord was with Joseph, and he [even though a slave] became a successful and prosperous man; and he was in the house of his master, the Egyptian."
Genesis 39:2 AMP

"For the husband is the head of the wife as Christ is the head of the church, his body, of which he is the Savior."
Ephesians 5:23 NIV

My Thoughts, Expectations, & Results:

_____

_____

_____

_____

_____

BLESSED CHILDREN

14. My children are blessed and favored by God. They are skillful, wise, and have value among kings.

"young men without blemish and handsome in appearance, skillful in all wisdom, endowed with intelligence and discernment, and quick to understand, competent to stand [in the presence of the king] and able to serve in the king's palace. He also ordered Ashpenaz to teach them the literature and language of the Chaldeans. Now God granted Daniel favor and compassion in the sight of the commander of the officials,"
Daniel 1:4, 9 AMP

My Thoughts, Expectations, & Results:

_____

_____

_____

_____

_____

VICTORY

15. My enemies will never triumph over me.

"By this I know that You favor and delight in me, Because my enemy does not shout in triumph over me."
Psalm 41:11 AMP

My Thoughts, Expectations, & Results:

_____

_____

_____

_____

_____

16. My family and I prosper in all areas of our lives, even in health.

"Beloved, I pray that in every way you may succeed and prosper and be in good health [physically], just as [I know] your soul prospers [spiritually]."
3 John 1:2 AMP

"I am about to go the way of all the earth," he said. "So be strong, act like a man, and observe what the Lord your God requires: Walk in obedience to him, and keep his decrees and commands, his laws and regulations, as written in the Law of Moses. Do this so that you may prosper in all you do and wherever you go and that the Lord may keep his promise to me: 'If your descendants watch how they live, and if they walk faithfully before me with all their heart and soul, you will never fail to have a successor on the throne of Israel."
1 Kings 2:2-4 NIV

My Thoughts, Expectations, & Results:

_____

_____

_____

_____

_____

HEALING

17. My family and I are walking miracles; therefore, infirmities shall never be our portion.

> *"The Lord will take away from you all sickness; and He will not subject you to any of the harmful diseases of Egypt which you have known, but He will impose them on all [those] who hate you."*
> **Deuteronomy 7:15 AMP**

My Thoughts, Expectations, & Results:

_____

_____

_____

_____

_____

POWER TO CREATE

18. I am wealthy because my Father in Heaven is the King of kings!

*"But you shall remember [with profound respect] the Lord
your God, for it is He who is giving you power to make
wealth, that He may confirm His covenant which He swore
(solemnly promised) to your fathers, as it is this day."*
Deuteronomy 8:18 AMP

My Thoughts, Expectations, & Results:

_____

_____

_____

_____

_____

DEBT-FREE

19. My family and I are debt-free.

"Then she came and told the man of God. He said, Go, sell the oil and pay your debt, and you and your sons live on the rest."
2 Kings 4:7 AMP

My Thoughts, Expectations, & Results:

_____

_____

_____

_____

_____

20. My household does not lack anything because we serve the Lord.

> *"Fear the Lord, you his holy people, for those who fear him lack nothing."*
> **Psalm 34:9 NIV**

My Thoughts, Expectations, & Results:

_____

_____

_____

_____

_____

POVERTY IS GONE

21. My household and bloodline will no longer experience poverty.

"However, there need be no poor people among you, for in the land the Lord your God is giving you to possess as your inheritance, he will richly bless you, if only you fully obey the Lord your God and are careful to follow all these commands I am giving you today."
Deuteronomy 5:4-5NIV

My Thoughts, Expectations, & Results:

_____

_____

_____

_____

_____

FAITH

22. My Faith in God will not fail me because it will only grow from here.

"It is written: "I believed; therefore I have spoken." Since we have that same spirit of faith, we also believe and therefore speak, because we know that the one who raised the Lord Jesus from the dead will also raise us with Jesus and present us with you to himself."
2 Corinthians 4:13-14 NIV

My Thoughts, Expectations, & Results:

_____

_____

_____

_____

_____

MULTIPLICATION

23. I am a landowner and faithful steward over everything added to me.

"Be careful to follow every command I am giving you today, so that you may live and increase and may enter and possess the land the Lord promised on oath to your ancestors."
Deuteronomy 8:1 NIV

"His master replied, 'Well done, good and faithful servant! You have been faithful with a few things; I will put you in charge of many things. Come and share your master's happiness!'
Matthew 25:23 NIV

My Thoughts, Expectations, & Results:

_____

_____

_____

_____

_____

24. The wisdom of God guilds me every day.

"Wisdom, like an inheritance, is a good thing and benefits those who see the sun. Wisdom is a shelter as money is a shelter, but the advantage of knowledge is this: Wisdom preserves those who have it."
Ecclesiastes 7:11-12 NIV

My Thoughts, Expectations, & Results:

_____

_____

_____

_____

_____

REAP

25. I abundantly reap all good things because I am a giver.

"Remember this: Whoever sows sparingly will also reap sparingly, and whoever sows generously will also reap generously."
2 Corinthians 9:6 NIV

My Thoughts, Expectations, & Results:

_____

_____

_____

_____

_____

STABILITY

26. My family and I are stable, with every need met by God.

"And my God will meet all your needs according to the riches of his glory in Christ Jesus."
Philippians 4:19 NIV

My Thoughts, Expectations, & Results:

_____

_____

_____

_____

_____

FRUITS

27. My spiritual fruits are mature and perfect in the sight of God.

"But the fruit of the Spirit is love, joy, peace, forbearance, kindness, goodness, faithfulness, gentleness and self-control. Against such things there is no law."
Galatians 5:22-23 NIV

My Thoughts, Expectations, & Results:

_____

_____

_____

_____

_____

LOVE

28. I am created in the image and likeness of God. Therefore, love is who I am.

"Love is patient, love is kind. It does not envy, it does not boast, it is not proud. It does not dishonor others, it is not self-seeking, it is not easily angered, it keeps no record of wrongs. Love does not delight in evil but rejoices with the truth. It always protects, always trusts, always hopes, always perseveres. Love never fails. But where there are prophecies, they will cease; where there are tongues, they will be stilled; where there is knowledge, it will pass away. And now these three remain: faith, hope and love. But the greatest of these is love."
1 Corinthians 13:4-8, 13 NIV

"So God created mankind in his own image, in the image of God he created them; male and female he created them."
Genesis 1:27 NIV

"Whoever has my commands and keeps them is the one who loves me. The one who loves me will be loved by my Father, and I too will love them and show myself to them."
John 14:21 NIV

My Thoughts, Expectations, & Results:

_____

_____

_____

SUBMIT

29. I find pleasure in submitting to God and my husband.

"Submit to one another out of reverence for Christ. Wives, submit yourselves to your own husbands as you do to the Lord."
Ephesians 5:21-22 NIV

My Thoughts, Expectations, & Results:

_____

_____

_____

_____

_____

HONORABLE MARRIAGE

30. My marriage is precious, sacred, and holy because God dwells in it.

> *"Marriage should be honored by all, and the marriage bed kept pure, for God will judge the adulterer and all the sexually immoral."*
> **Hebrews 13:4 NIV**

> *"So they are no longer two but one flesh. What therefore God has joined together, let not man separate."*
> **Matthew 19:6 ESV**

My Thoughts, Expectations, & Results:

_____

_____

_____

_____

_____

STRENGTH

31. I have the strength of the Lord that gets me through each test.

"I can do all things [which He has called me to do] through Him who strengthens and empowers me [to fulfill His purpose—I am self-sufficient in Christ's sufficiency; I am ready for anything and equal to anything through Him who infuses me with inner strength and confident peace]."
Philippians 4:13 AMP

My Thoughts, Expectations, & Results:

_____

_____

_____

_____

_____

PRAYER

Father, in the name of Yeshua,

Thank you for being Yahweh, Creator, Master, Lord, King, Daddy, etc. Thank you for never leaving us. Thank you for the love, mercy, patience, and grace you extend to us daily. Father, please forgive us for all the sins we commit. Forgive us for not bringing you glory. Please wash us with your blood to make us white as snow. Father, please open our eyes to understand right from wrong so we can be blameless in your sight. Open our ears to hear you when you call for us. God, please stand up in each woman reading this book to give them the confidence to walk boldly in their purpose. Please cover and protect each marriage, family, and business you have put together and commissioned them to manage. Father, help your daughters to understand why you have created them, and please reveal their purpose to them. Please give them the strategies they need to bring you glory. Lord, show your daughters why you created them to be a helpmeet in your Kingdom and assist them with the mission through your Holy Spirit. Help each of your daughters reading this book to know their worth and not settle for less in Yeshua's name, Amen!

www.ingramcontent.com/pod-product-compliance
Lightning Source LLC
Chambersburg PA
CBHW051600120626
46551CB00013B/1599